Dearest Lady Sonya —

I love you and I thank God for your ministry... may you always choose His Peace —

♡ Steffany

Philippians 4:7-8

The Choice Is Yours!

TIFFANY L. NELSON

Copyright © 2020 Tiffany L. Nelson.

All rights reserved. No part of this book may be used or reproduced by any means, graphic, electronic, or mechanical, including photocopying, recording, taping or by any information storage retrieval system without the written permission of the author except in the case of brief quotations embodied in critical articles and reviews.

This book is a work of non-fiction. Unless otherwise noted, the author and the publisher make no explicit guarantees as to the accuracy of the information contained in this book and in some cases, names of people and places have been altered to protect their privacy.

WestBow Press books may be ordered through booksellers or by contacting:

WestBow Press
A Division of Thomas Nelson & Zondervan
1663 Liberty Drive
Bloomington, IN 47403
www.westbowpress.com
844-714-3454

Because of the dynamic nature of the Internet, any web addresses or links contained in this book may have changed since publication and may no longer be valid. The views expressed in this work are solely those of the author and do not necessarily reflect the views of the publisher, and the publisher hereby disclaims any responsibility for them.

Any people depicted in stock imagery provided by Getty Images are models, and such images are being used for illustrative purposes only.
Certain stock imagery © Getty Images.

Scripture quotations marked KJV are taken from the King James Version.

ISBN: 978-1-6642-1180-3 (sc)
ISBN: 978-1-6642-1181-0 (e)

Library of Congress Control Number: 2020922103

Print information available on the last page.

WestBow Press rev. date: 12/15/2020

To my Lord and Savior, Jesus Christ, first and foremost, without whom none of this would be possible. He placed a yearning in my heart to give voice to thoughts, and He has become my muse and my inspiration.

To my loving husband, Fred Nelson, who brings me joy beyond measure and is my biggest fan; my two children, Jazlynn Christine and Miles Anthony, who fuel my passion for life; my mother, Phyllis Davis, who introduced me to reading at an early age and fostered my love affair with words; my wonderful father, Cornelius Davis, who even when he knew the answer to my question would make me research the encyclopedia for the answer; and my beloved brothers, Eric and Phillip, who have always allowed me to be their big sister in every sense of the word; and to everyone who has ever encouraged me to write and share my gift, this book is humbly dedicated to each of you.

Contents

Introduction ix
Chapter 1   The Million-Dollar Question 1
Chapter 2   Who Says You Have to Accept It? 5
Chapter 3   Excuses! Excuses! 9
Chapter 4   Imagine 13
Chapter 5   An Opportunity of a Lifetime......................17
Chapter 6   Grace and Mercy 21
Chapter 7   Get Up from There!.....................................25
Chapter 8   Only Believe 29
Chapter 9   Proper Alignment 33
Chapter 10   The Power of Your Choice 37
Chapter 11   Sweet Surrender 41

Introduction

The power of choice is a force to be reckoned with indeed. Sometimes we forget that we actually have a choice in the matter. We do not have to stay where we are. We do not have to remain in relationships that no longer bring us joy. We do not have to become who others say we are. We do not have to accept mediocrity. We do not have to walk around with our heads in the ground. We do not have to live lives full of guilt and shame. And furthermore, we do not have to allow our weaknesses and challenges in life to define who we are.

Life happens to us all. Sometimes things that happen are completely out of our control. Not one of us is immune to pain and suffering. At some point, we all will experience the highs and lows of life. We all will lose someone we love. Undoubtedly, someone will make a mess in our lives and leave us behind to clean it up. Sometimes bad things happen to good people. Sometimes there is no human explanation as to how we ended up where we are. And sometimes it's not even our fault.

But in spite of whatever has happened, understand that it is not the end of your story. The Lord Himself is the author and finisher of your faith. You are not alone. Your dreams are not washed up. You yet have purpose. God still has a plan for your life. He wants to lift your spirit and take you to a higher place in Him. You have not slipped beneath His radar. He has always known exactly where you are. He has felt every one of your emotions, and, beloved, He has bottled every tear you have ever cried.

There is a time and a season for all things, and as God would have it, seasons change. No one season lasts forever. Today can be the first day of the rest of your life. Today can be the day you experience the miraculous workings of Christ in you and through you. You do not have to live another day beneath God's plan and purpose for your life. The pain and heartache that has gripped every fiber of your being can be released today. You can begin life anew. You can put the past behind you, where it belongs, and step into your rightful place of victory. But it's up to you. The Choice is Yours!

As we begin to explore the powerful healing and restoration in the life of a man mentioned in the Gospel of John 5:1–9, I pray that your faith will be renewed by the matchless power of Jesus Christ. I pray that you will be strengthened to confidently walk away from everything and everyone who has held you hostage. I pray that you will no longer be passive in your pursuit of happiness and that you will allow God to erase every lie Satan has ever told you. I speak peace and restoration over your life and blessings in Christ that you can't begin to imagine.

Are you ready? Let's begin.

> After this there was a feast of the Jews; and Jesus went up to Jerusalem. Now there is at Jerusalem by the sheep market a pool, which is called in the Hebrew tongue Bethesda, having five porches. In these lay a great

multitude of impotent folk, of blind, halt, withered, waiting for the moving of the water. For an angel went down at a certain season into the pool, and troubled the water: whosoever then first after the troubling of the water stepped in was made whole of whatsoever disease he had.

And a certain man was there, which had an infirmity thirty and eight years. When Jesus saw him lie, and knew that he had been now a long time in that case, He saith unto him, Wilt thou be made whole? The impotent man answered him, Sir, I have no man, when the water is troubled, to put me into the pool: but while I am coming, another steppeth down before me.

Jesus saith unto him, Rise, take up thy bed, and walk. And immediately the man was made whole, and took up his bed, and walked: and the same day was the Sabbath. (John 5:1–9 KJV)

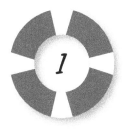

The Million-Dollar Question

Jesus asked the impotent man a simple question: "Wilt thou be made whole?" (John 5:6 KJV). Now, as far as I'm concerned, that was a straightforward question that should have been answered with a resounding *yes*. Or so you might think. But when you take a closer look from the man's point of view, perhaps there was a reason he answered Jesus in the way he did.

Have you ever stood in plain sight and felt utterly invisible? It is interesting that the writer of this Gospel does not refer to this man by name but rather a label. A name gives identity. It tells who you are and who you come from. When people call your name, it means that they see you or recognize your presence. Yet he is referred to only as "the impotent man." Immediately, I envision a man, possibly impoverished, extremely feeble, physically and emotionally weathered, ungroomed, and unsightly.

My vision of this man, however, says nothing of his character but only of his circumstance. Some of us know exactly how it feels to be labeled because of our lots in life. People have long since stopped calling us by our names, and all we hear now are whispers: She's a widow. He's a divorcé. She's a home-wrecker. She's a mother with a young son in jail. She's a welfare recipient. He's homeless. She's a middle-aged, overweight woman. She's a single mom, and all of her children have different fathers. He's a dropout. She's depressed. He's a nobody—the list goes on and on.

Although you can't control the thoughts and words of others, you can most definitely control your thoughts and your words. If you are not careful, before long, instead of living up to your name, you will live under the label.

I imagine most of us are hesitant to admit it, but we each know a little something about powerlessness. Powerlessness can make you forget who you are. It takes hold of your identity and silences you in ways you might never imagine. Powerlessness is a dream-killer. It leaves you feeling helpless. It exaggerates your inadequacies. It can make you feel useless, good for nothing—or simply invisible.

Perhaps that's why it is not so surprising that the man did not readily realize that it was the All-Powerful asking him not only if he wanted to feel better but if he wanted to be made whole. Until recently, I stood in sharp judgment of this man. I have always thought, *How pathetic is that? Jesus is offering him the chance of a lifetime, and all he can come up with is a big, fat excuse. Really?*

Instead of screaming an emphatic *yes*, he tells Jesus of his plight: he has no one to help him into the pool, and although he recognizes that it is his season to make a move, everyone else seems to move faster. They not only beat him to the punch;

they leave him lying there, stuck in the same place! My heart begins to soften as I consider his words.

Can you imagine your dream within arm's reach but not having the physical strength to reach out and grab it? Can you imagine the frustration of being so close to everything you have ever wanted, yet being so far away? I can almost see the tears in his eyes—hot, jealous, angry, hopeless tears. Tears that scream, "Why don't you just give up? It's pointless to keep trying! No one wants to help you. It won't get any better. This is how it will always be. You were never destined for greatness. Settle down. Make yourself comfortable. Face the facts—you will die here!"

Wow. What painful tears to cry. The sharp judgment I once felt begins to dissipate, and I can feel my heart softening toward him. Sometimes, when you have been down for so long or at a disadvantage for so long, it is hard to imagine anything else. Undoubtedly, he wanted to be better—we all want to be better—but all he could see was his circumstance. Jesus was offering him a way out. And Jesus is offering *you* a way out.

Who Says You Have to Accept It?

Believe it or not, you do *not* have to accept where you are right now. Just because you fall down does not mean that you are weak and lack the ability to stand. Just because you've tried and failed does not inherently make you a failure. Perhaps you have physical challenges, but having those physical challenges does not mean you are, by default, intellectually challenged. Too often, we accept what Satan throws our way, and because it appears to be out of our control, we figure that this is the way it has to be.

The impotent man in John 5:1–9 suffered a severe handicap for perhaps the better part of his life. There was nothing he could do to change the condition of his body. He did not have an easy life. I imagine he was not voted most popular and that, growing up, he probably never was chosen to be a part of anyone's team. He never heard anybody say, "I want to be just like him when I grow up," because no one wanted to be like him; truth be told, even *he* did not want to be him.

As the years went by—thirty-eight years, to be exact—I imagine it became easier to accept that he would never walk again, that he would always require the assistance of someone else, that he would never be gainfully employed, and that he would never know the joys of having physical strength and agility. Undoubtedly, when he looked at his life, he uttered those words that are all too familiar to many of us: it is what it is. Even though he did not like his situation, and it left him feeling empty, alone, and miserable, over the years, sadly, he learned to just accept it.

Every day was the same old thing. Each new day chipped away at the hope of the future he desired. Although he was at a place where great miracles were happening right before his eyes, the only thing he had was more misery, more pain, anguish, and disillusionment—never a miracle. Even though he was at the right place, it never seemed to be the right time. He needed help. He couldn't do it by himself.

Think about it: it took a lot to even get to the marketplace. It was indeed a struggle—not just a physical struggle but also a psychological struggle. Can you imagine how much harder it became, year after year, to drag himself to the marketplace and then to not be able to get inside the pool? Even though his miracle was within arm's reach, it must have felt as though it was a thousand miles away.

Have you ever been there? Have you ever felt stuck? Do you ever wonder, *What's the use?* Have you ever asked yourself, "Why should I bother getting out of bed?" Or "Why should I bother showing up?" Be honest. Have you ever said, "Nothing has changed"? Maybe you've said, "I haven't changed. The situation hasn't changed. I've done all that I can do. No one is willing to help me. Help is not on the way. My life is doomed. It's a wrap. I give up!"

My friend, you could not be more wrong. You may not have the answers today; you may not have the resources today. Maybe today, you still feel the same way you did yesterday and the day before and the day before that. But have you forgotten that you have a choice in the matter? Who says you have to accept things the way they are? Who's to say that things will not get better? You don't have to lie there or stand there or wait there or be pitiful there or be hopeless there for another moment.

Maybe you have been to every physician or spoken with every therapist or taken every kind of medication there is to take, and you have seen no change. Don't give up! Sometimes, what we truly need goes beyond the physicality of our circumstances. I challenge your faith today. I dare you to *not* accept things as they are. I dare you to dream again. I dare you to grab hold of faith the size of a mustard seed. Even if it feels like your situation is half-past dead, hope again!

Jesus is knocking at the doors of your heart. Can you hear Him? He is not like the people around you. He sees you. He feels your pain. He knows your case. He's here to help. "But Jesus beheld them, and said unto them, With men this is impossible; but with God all things are possible" (Matthew 19:26 KJV).

Excuses! Excuses!

Not every excuse is a lie. Sometimes our excuses are absolutely true, as in the case of this man who sat beside the pool. It is true that everybody saw him sitting there. Everybody knew the pitiful condition he was in. Everybody realized that the only way he could ever get into the pool was if one of them helped him.

It is really quite amazing how people can see you, yet not *see* you. They can see the tears in your eyes and the strain upon your brow, yet they refuse to feel your pain, and they do absolutely nothing to lighten your load. These are the people who watched the dissolution of your marriage. They saw your wayward child behave recklessly. They had front-row seats to your being overlooked and completely disregarded. They have seen the disrespect. They have seen the abuse. They see that you have all but fallen to the ground, and they do *nothing*.

This can be a bitter pill to swallow. Anger sets in, and before long, you find yourself mad at everyone, and excuses become the name of the game. Do any of the following excuses sound familiar?

I would be further along *if* …

I could have been great, *but* …

I could be happy, *if* it weren't for …

I could be pretty *if* …

I could really praise God *if* things were different.

The only reason I am still sitting here is …

It's not my fault;

It's my spouse's fault.

It's my parents' fault.

It's the church's fault.

My spouse died.

They promoted someone else.

The stock market dropped.

My spouse left me for someone younger.

Yes, it happened. Yes, it was real. No, you did not imagine it. And no, you cannot use any of it to justify why you have chosen not to walk into your destiny. Think about it—does your excuse change anything? Does it alter the reality that stares you in the face every morning? Does it make you feel any better? Wouldn't you agree that it is time to flip the script on your circumstances? It's time to stop allowing your circumstances to dictate how you live your life. Instead of allowing your circumstances to bully you, take back your power and declare victory—no matter how it looks, no matter how it feels, no matter what the naysayers think or say. Declare victory!

I know it's easier said than done. Year after year, the scenario was always the same for the impotent man. Each year brought the same disappointment, the same frustration, and the same outcome. I can imagine how powerless he felt as the years went by. I can almost feel his hopelessness slipping like sand through an hourglass. When Jesus asked him the life-changing question—"Wilt thou be made whole?"—he responded, "Sir, I have no man, when the water is troubled, to put me into the pool: but while I am coming, another steppeth down before me" (John 5:6–7 KJV).

Notice that Jesus did not ask him *why* he was sitting there. Rather, the man was asked if he wanted to be made whole—two totally different questions. The impotent man was so consumed with his physical condition and lack of physical strength that he was unable to hear what Jesus really asked. He also felt the need to tell Jesus that not only did the others refuse to help him, but they also beat him to the pool every time.

I get it. He was frustrated. He was tired. He was at his wit's end. Undoubtedly, he was used to being judged by his condition. Like most of us, he did not want to be in that situation, and he certainly did not ask for it. But there he was.

He was so used to nobody helping him that he did not even realize that someone, who was willing and able to help him beyond what he could ever imagine, was standing right there in front of him. That someone was offering more than just healing; Jesus was offering to make him whole from the inside out. The answer to his lifelong prayer was right there, staring him in the face.

Imagine

I challenge you to dream again. Dreams are powerful and sometimes are the very catalysts we need to shift and reshape our realities.

What if there is something more out there? What if this present trial is not the last stop on the road for you?

Consider some of the great, influential people who have since passed on. Each of them had a dream. What got them through the *now* was the prospect of the future. They were not blind to the reality of their circumstances, but they dreamed of a better, brighter day. They may have been downtrodden at one point, but they somehow imagined that victory was just beyond the horizon. They suffered from lack, but they could see abundance farther up the road.

Despite what you are faced with today, you yet have every reason to hope for better days—days filled with more laughter and more joy; days filled with blessings and contentment beyond anything you can imagine; days where there are fewer struggles and greater achievements. Close your eyes for a moment. Quiet your spirit. I give you permission to forget about all your current struggles and everything that has you down. I give you permission to push aside every negative thought and every negative emotion. You owe it to yourself. For the next few moments, give yourself a much-deserved break from it all.

A dear childhood friend of mine stands before his congregation and regularly reminds them, "You have to see it before you see it." To some, that may sound catchy or glib, but the very reason it is not is because he is a blind man who pastors a sighted church. He challenges them to become blind to what they see and to reach for what they do not see so that they can envision the life they dream of. If you can dream it, you can someday achieve it. Sometimes, those without sight have clearer vision than those of us who can see. Through faith, you can begin to see past the darkness that stares you in the face every day without allowing that darkness to kill your dream.

Use your imagination. Let your imagination run wild and free. Resist the urge to focus on your heartache, pain, illness, ailments, disappointment, disability, frustration, lack of finances, or unemployment. Give yourself permission to imagine something different. It's hard; I get it. I have been there—more than once. Grief nearly swallowed my heart whole. Losing my first spouse and being left alone to raise an eighteen-month-old and a nearly three-year-old was a daunting prospect, to say the least. It was hard for me to imagine the next few minutes, let alone the next few years.

My husband and I were young. I never thought about being a widow at thirty-nine. I never thought cancer would come knocking at our door. I did not sign up to be a single mother. I had seen countless other women do it, but could I do it? How could I raise my eighteen-month-old son to be a man? After all, I'm a woman. I felt stuck. I felt sad. I felt that no one understood my pain. I felt that no one could see the tears tracing my cheeks. I felt that no one could see that my heart was shredded into pieces and bleeding profusely.

The man at the pool encountered this same difficulty. It had to be hard for him to imagine running when he couldn't even walk. It had to be hard for him to imagine gainful employment, or meeting the love of his life, or being respectable in the eyes of those around him, when he couldn't even pick himself up. Thirty-eight years is a long time to be without a dream.

It is important to understand that your *imagination* may not always match *reality*. And this is probably a good thing, especially when our imaginations drop us off in a dark place. The gift of imagination can be our saving grace. It keeps us alive. It keeps us striving and thriving. It takes us from a mere black-and-white existence into a full Technicolor experience!

Your imagination allows you to be whoever you want to be. You get to dictate how your life looks and how it feels. There are no boundaries. There are no rules. There are no obstacles—just you and your wildest dreams.

What are you *not* dreaming about?

An Opportunity of a Lifetime

Jesus uttered these five life-changing words: "Wilt thou be made whole?" (John 5:6 KJV). Who would ever imagine that something with which he had struggled with for thirty-eight years could come to an end with just five simple words?

He was five words away from his struggle being over. Five words away from being able to walk. Five words away from leaping and running. Five words away from escaping misery and shame. Five words away from being at the mercy of others. He was five words away from being independent and experiencing the freedom to become who he was created to be. He was five words away from his dream becoming reality.

When you are in the throes of extreme hardship or sickness for an extended period of time, it can honestly feel like forever. Year after year, appointment after appointment, hearing the same *no*, stuck in the same pitiful position, continuously being dismissed and overlooked can be crushing and leave you feeling like this must be your lot in life. Why even bother imagining something different? This is it. It is what it is.

Thirty-eight years of powerlessness can leave a mark on you. Thirty-eight years of sitting at the same place, watching others walk into their victories as you shrink in the shadows, can play cruel tricks on your mind. I can almost hear the impotent man ask himself, "Is this real? Am I real? Am I invisible? Do they really not see me? Do they really not care? How can they leave me sitting here like this? Is there no human decency? Is there no care and consideration for your fellow man? Am I not good enough? Am I not worthy enough? Am I really this pathetic?" So he did what a lot of people do with seemingly unsurmountable circumstances: he became stuck where he was. He resolved to just sit there.

Have you ever been there? I have. Seems like every time you pull yourself up, something bigger, stronger, and nastier pulls you back down. You try to do the right thing, you try to play by the rules, but instead of people lifting you up, they tear you down. You come to church with tears in your eyes, but your fellow parishioners act as though they can't see the tears tracing your cheeks. They shake your hand, exchange niceties, and ask how you are doing, but they move on to the next person before you can even answer.

After a while, you stop looking for a hand up. It stops crossing your mind that there is still human decency in the world. You stop looking in the mail. You stop waiting for that phone call. You stop hoping for that positive test result. You stop dreaming. You stop writing. You stop singing. You stop reaching. And it isn't long before you have even stopped praying. You no longer believe. And all you can say is, "It is what it is."

THE CHOICE IS YOURS!

But what if it's not? What if today is different? What if today is the first day of your new life? What if today is the day that God has ordained to be the day of miracles and manifestation in your life? There is a time and a season for all things. What if today is your day? What if today is the day you hear that knock at the door? What if the one thing you have stopped praying for is on the other side of that door?

The impotent man had no idea how his life was about to change. He had no idea who was speaking to him. Undoubtedly, he woke up that morning, feeling as though that day would be like every other day. Little did he know that he was about to come face-to-face with an opportunity of a lifetime. He would soon realize that he was not invisible. Someone had seen his struggle. Someone had felt his pain. Someone cared enough to ask him how he was doing. Someone cared enough to listen to his response.

That day was the last day he would have to worry about getting to the pool. Living Water had come to meet him, right where he was. This someone was not just anyone. This someone was more than a listening ear. This someone was more than just someone who was familiar with his situation. This particular someone not only had compassion but unlimited power to do extraordinary things.

More than just a physical healing, Jesus offered the impotent man wholeness from the inside out. Wholeness would bring about healing from all of the invisible cuts and scars. Wholeness would penetrate deeper than his legs. Wholeness would bring healing to his soul. Sometimes, we focus on what our eyes can see. We tell ourselves that if this were different or that were different, if we didn't have this or if didn't have that, our lives would be so much better. But Jesus looked beyond the man's physical condition and perceived his true need.

Sometimes, what we really need—even more than a new house, a new car, a new job, more money in the bank, or even a healing from a dreadful disease—is emotional and spiritual healing. Our true needs often run deeper than we realize. What good is a new body without a new mind? Having a new perspective transcends anything we experience in the natural.

You have heard the expression, "Father knows best." Our heavenly Father absolutely knows what is best for us. He created us and therefore knows everything there is to know about us. He knows we do not *need* everything we want. We look at the surface. He looks at the root. We focus on getting ahead. He focuses on propelling us toward our destinies.

Grace and Mercy

Thankfully, there is no place we travel in life where God will not send grace and mercy to follow us. One of the things I have come to love most about my heavenly Father is that He has broad shoulders. He can stand my not understanding His will for my life. He can handle my being upset with Him. He can bear the brunt of being momentarily misunderstood. He can even handle it when I give Him the silent treatment by refusing to pray and share my heart with Him.

God's grace is sufficient, even when you can't perceive it, even when you can't perceive Him. No matter what you go through in life or what He allows you to suffer and endure, God's grace is sufficient. God loves you in spite of you. He loves you when you love Him back and loves you still when you turn your back to Him and walk away. He even loves you when you toss Him in the box with everyone else who has ever failed or disappointed you.

The impotent man who was not given the common

courtesy of assistance was offered unmerited favor from Jesus Himself. Even though he did not readily recognize Jesus, Jesus knew exactly who the man was and how long he had been sitting there. Even though the man had undoubtedly given up on his dream to walk again, grace appeared unto him, along with mercy, forgiving him and restoring everything he had lost.

The grace of God covers our shortcomings. The grace of God lifts us when life attempts to keep us down. The grace of God gives us strength to continue forward in the midst of chaos and disappointment. God's mercy covers our sin; covers our indiscretions; covers our unbelief. Instead of throwing the book at us, mercy forgives, forgets, and restores us to our rightful place. God's mercy does not give us what we deserve but rather gives us His good pleasure.

Jesus asks the man if he wants to be made whole. Instead of saying yes, the impotent man starts in with excuses. Instead of answering a direct question, he begins shifting the blame to everyone else. Jesus was not asking him what everyone else was doing. For the first time in thirty-eight years, it was all about him, only he did not realize it. They say it's hard to teach an old dog new tricks. He had become a victim of his circumstance. Even so, Jesus extended grace and mercy.

As you read the pages of this book, I feel in my spirit as though Jesus is extending grace and mercy to you. He is not mad at you. He has not turned His back on you. He is not out to get you. He loves you, and His thoughts toward you are peaceful. Yes, you may have stopped praying. Yes, you may have stopped believing. Yes, you may have nearly given up on Him, but He has never stopped wanting to be in a relationship with you. He has never stopped believing in you. He has never given up on you—nor will He ever.

THE CHOICE IS YOURS!

There is a reason behind your trial. There is purpose beneath your pain. The tears were necessary. The waiting was necessary. Nothing about what you have been through is arbitrary. You may never completely understand the 'why' but that's because God wants you to know the 'who' behind it all. Even though He could be mad, or inflict punishment, or cast you away, He instead showers you with grace. At this moment, God is knocking at the door of your heart. Can you hear Him?

Today really is your day. Right now is your moment. Life as you know it can begin anew. Everything else around you may be the same, but you can be different. Seize this opportunity. Receive His grace and mercy.

The same question is asked of you that Jesus asked of the impotent man: "Wilt thou be made whole?" Are you going to blame everything and everyone else? Are you going to shift the focus from you? Will you recognize who is speaking to your heart? Will you acknowledge that despite how difficult it has been, God's grace has sustained you? Are you ready to thank Him that your sanity is still intact? Are you willing to accept the unmerited favor He is offering you?

My friend, are you tired of being tired? Have you had enough of not having enough? Are you ready to dream again? Are you ready to live life to the fullest? I know you are! Answer the door. Jesus is on the other side of that door. Everything you need is waiting outside that door and is yours for the opening.

Give prayer another try. Getting to the door will not be easy. It will take a lot of strength and a lot of effort to get there, but grace and mercy are there to carry you and hold you up. They will even walk alongside of you. Your spirit may feel a little weary and wobbly, but God's all-sufficient grace is all you need to propel you toward your mark. Trust Him.

Get Up from There!

Now is no time for excuses. You cannot deny the knocking you hear at your heart. The presence of almighty God is undeniable. Jesus asks the impotent man a life-changing question: "Wilt thou be made whole?" (John 5:6 KJV), to which he answers, "Sir, I have no man, when the water is troubled, to put me into the pool: but while I am coming, another steppeth down before me" (John 5:7 KJV). My friend, the struggle is indeed real. Can you imagine the immensity of his plight? He uses every bit of the little strength he has to press toward the pool, only to watch others zoom past him and get there first—and not just this day but year after year.

To his credit, he never stopped trying. After thirty-eight years, it would be easy to see why anyone would give up trying altogether. Thirty-eight years is a long time. It's a long time to believe. It's a long time to hope. And even though his response to Jesus may sound like nothing more than an excuse, it was his truth. His energy and effort were of no consequence. Each time, he met with the same outcome. Every year that passed represented another year of defeat, another year of exasperation, another year that no one cared enough about him to help him reach his destiny.

And so he probably figured, *Why would this year or this season be any different from all the others?* I am sure it was nice that, at least in this season, someone actually took note of him, spoke to him, and was nice enough to ask him about his life and well-being, but would it really change anything?

Has this ever happened to you? Someone will ask, "How are you doing?" But before you can answer, he or she has already walked past you. Or maybe someone will ask how you are doing and actually will give you the time and space to share your heart, but when you finish, all that person says is, "Wow. I am so sorry to hear that, but hang in there." He or she walks away, leaving you feeling no different from when that person first came. It can truly be disheartening, to say the least.

But little did this man know that the one to whom he was speaking was no regular, run-of-the-mill kind of guy. This was no ordinary exchange between two men. Little did he know that this moment was divinely appointed unto him. The impotent man had spent thirty-eight years focused on getting himself to the pool, which had caused him nothing but extreme frustration, fatigue, and vexation of his spirit, when all the while, all he really needed was to get to Jesus.

Jesus *is* the troubling in the water because He *is* Living Water. Jesus is the one who heals our bodies and our minds and our hearts. Jesus is the one who delivers us from sin, breaks the chains that bind us, and sets us free. In this man's case, it was not about the pool, or his lack of physical strength, or the lack of help from his fellow man. It was all about having an encounter with Jesus. So Jesus, being fully aware of the man's thirty-eight-year struggle, speaks seven one-syllable words with enough power to change this poor man's life forever.

Jesus says, "Rise, take up thy bed, and walk" (John 5:8 KJV). In my own mind, I hear, *Get up from there!* My friend, there is power behind and within every word that Jesus speaks. When He speaks, demons tremble. When He speaks, things change and people change. When He speaks, there is a shifting in the atmosphere; our circumstances begin to shift, pieces of the puzzle begin to shift, and our faith begins to shift to another dimension.

The scripture says, "And immediately the man was made whole, and took up his bed, and walked" (John 5:9 KJV). Did you catch that? *Immediately*—not the next day, not the following week, but at that very moment, without hesitation, without second-guessing the command, he was made whole. As quickly as he obeyed, he was made whole—that very second—from the inside out. What a difference faith and obedience make in our lives! He went from lying down to standing up, from standing up to walking, and from walking to declaring his miracle. He had been pitifully lying down for thirty-eight long years, and now he had strength to pick up his bed, tuck it under his arm, and walk anywhere and everywhere he wanted.

Perhaps when you first read John's account of the impotent man, you immediately thought you did not want to be anything like him. But in the spirit, I feel a shift taking place for you, as it did for me. Despite everything he had suffered and endured—physically, emotionally, and spiritually—the impotent man obeyed the voice of Jesus. When he was told to get up, he got up. Just like that! He made no more excuses. He stopped rehashing the past. He forgot about his weakness and simply obeyed the command. Jesus met him right where he was. And just like that, he was not only healed but made whole.

To what have you been reaching to get? What seems so close and yet so far away? About what thing have you told yourself that if you can get to it, your life will be so much better? My friend, change your focus. More than things, more than a promotion, more than finances, more than anything else you are trying to get to, make sure that you get to Christ! Stop looking at resources, and tap into the source. Jesus is the source from whence all blessings flow. Rise up from mediocrity. Rise up from the pit of despair. Rise up from defeat. Exchange the spirit of heaviness for a garment of praise. Come on. You can do it. Get up from there!

Only Believe

Believing is 80 percent of the battle. If you can see it, you can become it. You can experience it. Can you see yourself as healed? Can you see yourself as a best-selling author? Can you see yourself as a recording artist? Can you see yourself as full of courage, proclaiming the Word of God in other regions of the world? Can you see yourself as living without fear, guilt, and shame? Can you see yourself as financially stable? Can you see yourself as living your best life? Well, believing that you can is the first big step toward what God has for you. So many times, we doubt ourselves. We doubt our abilities, and we doubt that we have the necessary fortitude to bring our dreams to fruition.

Rebuilding your life and operating in the dream is hard work. Passivity has no place in the process. A new life or a realized dream will not simply fall from the sky into your lap. There will be blood, sweat, and tears along the way. Not everyone will believe in you. Not everyone will trust or understand the vision. Yes, there will be haters; expect them—people who are jealous and intimidated by the greatness they see in you.

(This calls for a pause: if *they* can see the greatness inside you, why can't you see the greatness inside yourself?)

There will be days where the vision is ever so sweet, with everything falling into its rightful place, and then there will be days filled with so much darkness and uncertainty, where you cannot even see the dream—or see God, for that matter. There will be nights when you entertain lies from the enemy; nights when his diabolical antics make you want to give up and throw in the towel and stay stuck where you are.

But the good news is that 80 percent of the battle is simply believing who God is and what He has the power to do through you. If you continue thinking that *you* have to do all of it and God none of it, you will remain overwhelmed. What you need at this very moment is a divine attitude adjustment. The only thing God requires of you is obedience and faith. He will take care of the rest. It is imperative that you develop a yes-I-can mentality.

For years, you may have quoted, "I can do all things through Christ who strengtheneth me" (Philippians 4:13 KJV). Well, now it's time to *believe* it! How many times have you quoted, "Now unto Him that is able to do exceeding, abundantly above all that we ask or think, according to the power that worketh in us" (Ephesians 3:20 KJV)? But do you truly *believe* His Word? These are not feel-good words that leave us feeling warm and fuzzy. These God-inspired words are the keys that unlock our blessings.

When I was growing up, the old folks had a saying: "Much prayer much power; little prayer little power; no prayer no power." What level of power are you working with? Your prayers have wings. Your prayers have power. Prayer will help you maintain a clear mind. You must believe God beyond your five senses. Turn off your peripheral view and focus solely upon God. Focus on His character. God is omniscient, meaning He is all-knowing. Nothing you do or ever have done takes Him by surprise. God is omnipotent, meaning He is all-powerful. He has no limits. There is nothing He cannot do. God is omnipresent, meaning He is everywhere at the same time. You are never outside His reach or view. Wherever you think you are going, He is already there.

You can believe God because He is all-powerful. He can back up His Word. He cannot lie; it is literally impossible for Him to lie. He speaks it, and it comes into existence. God said, "Let there be light" (Genesis 1:3 KJV), and there was light. He has the power to call things that are not as if they were. He can do anything! Do you believe that God is faithful? Do you believe that His Word is truth? If He has placed a longing for something more in your spirit, believe it, speak it, and wait for manifestation—it's coming! My friend, "With God, all things are possible, if only you *believe*" (Matthew 19:26 KJV).

9

Proper Alignment

Alignment with the will of God for your life is everything. Many times, what we want and what we need are two very different things. Sometimes, our motives and intentions are in the wrong place. Sometimes, we foolishly think we know what is best for us, based on what we see and what we feel. We waste precious time with praying for things that are not in God's will for our lives, which will only bring us unnecessary pain and suffering.

Maybe you are praying for a spouse, and over the years, you have created a long laundry list of characteristics and attributes that he or she needs to have. But how much time have you spent preparing yourself for your future mate? Have you ever considered that your future spouse also wants God's best?

Singlehood is not a curse; it is a gift. Use this time to align yourself with the will of God. First and foremost, God desires to be in a relationship with you. He wants to be your first thought. He wants to be the one you run to when trouble strikes. He wants your honesty and your truth. He loves you and utterly adores you. He wants the best for you and has it to give to you. All He asks in return is that you love Him with all of your heart and with all of your soul (Deuteronomy 6:5 KJV).

Everything that has happened and is currently taking place is by design. Imagine that! You are actually right where God wants you to be. Is it comfortable? No. Is it ideal? Probably not. But is it necessary? Absolutely yes! Tragedy and trials have a way of bringing us to our knees in humble submission to God. Strangely, losing what we treasure most helps us to gain perspective. It forces us to reevaluate our state of mind and our existence.

It took me years to realize the key to unlocking my blessings. For most of my life, I had gone about it all wrong. I relied on my own wisdom—or lack thereof. I thought if I were pretty enough, perfect enough, or thin enough, that my heart's desire would fall from the sky. But that only left me even more frustrated, so I finally did what I should have done years before: I began to pray from a sincere place.

I asked God, "What am I doing wrong?" God works in mysterious ways. One day, while perusing my social media account, I stumbled across a cartoon illustration that changed my perspective; maybe you have seen it too. Jesus is on bended knee in front of a little girl, who is holding a small teddy bear in her arms. Jesus has one arm extended to her, as if asking for her bear, and one arm behind His back, hiding a big teddy bear. The little girl is saying, "But I love it." His words to her are a gentle reminder that she should trust Him. She has no idea what He plans to give her in exchange.

I was that little girl. I was holding on to something that could not compare with what God had in store for me. I was willing to settle for the little I was holding. Wow—imagine God speaking through social media. The Holy Spirit directed me to read what has since become one of my favorite verses: "And this is the confidence that we have in Him, that, if we ask anything according to His will, He heareth us. And if we know that He heareth us, whatsoever we ask, we know that we have the petitions that we desire of Him" (1 John 5:14–15 KJV).

It wasn't until I aligned my desires with His desire for my life that I began to experience manifestation. First, I had to come to the end of my rope. My blessing had been standing right in front of my face, but I was too blind to see it because it didn't appear as I thought it should have. But little by little, I gained enough strength to place my tiny teddy bear aside, and before I knew it, I was holding the biggest, cuddliest, most lovable teddy bear—whom I now call *husband*!

I believe that the impotent man had come to the end of his rope as well. He needed a change. He was willing to do whatever it took to usher in that change. God knows how much we can bear. He knows when we have come to the end of ourselves. He knows when we have exhausted every ounce of our human effort, and that's when He steps in. It's not until then that we are ready to trust Him and go all the way with Him. The impotent man had had enough of his pitiful condition, and that's when Jesus appeared to him out of nowhere.

We sing a song at my church called "He's an On-Time God," by Dottie Peoples: "He may not come when you want Him, but He will be there right on time." No lyrics ever have rung truer! God is on time. He is never late. He is never early.

He simply is. Although the impotent man initially offered excuses, something deep inside him felt compelled to obey the command of Jesus. What did he have to lose? He pushed aside his excuses. He pushed beyond his past. His lack of physical strength no longer mattered. In that moment, he believed. He aligned himself with the will of God. Jesus said, "Rise" (John 5:8 KJV), and he did exactly that. Obedience and faith will bring you into proper alignment every time.

The Power of Your Choice

At your weakest point, you still have the incredible superpower of choice. When you realize that you actually have a say in the matter, that is the day your life will change dramatically. Far too often, we allow our mountains to speak to us, but, my friend, I challenge you to speak to your mountain!

Life happens to us all, but how we choose to live our lives is up to us. Sometimes, we are too afraid to make a choice. We are afraid that we will make the wrong choice. We are afraid of potential repercussions. We are afraid that we will fail. But therein lies the paradox of choice—*not* choosing is still a choice.

More often than not, we cannot change our circumstances, but we can change ourselves. This is critical to grasp. You cannot change the heart of someone and make that person love you or help you. That's his or her business. But you can take a long look in the mirror and change the reflection that stares back at you.

Instead of waiting for someone to speak to you and validate you, speak to yourself. Choose to encourage yourself. Choose to be kind to yourself. Choose to be your own biggest fan. Choose to be positive. Instead of defeat and negativity, choose *joy*. Choose *happiness*. Choose to build your self-esteem. Tell yourself that your present condition is temporary. I don't care how long it's been that way; remind yourself that it is only temporary. Maybe the love of your life walked out and said, "I don't love you anymore." Maybe you came to work, only to discover that your position had been terminated.

Maybe you have received unfavorable news from the doctor. Maybe there is nothing more that medicine can do. Maybe the doctor said, "This your new normal, so deal with it." The bills are piling as high as the ceiling, and your bank account has long ago dipped below zero. All eyes are upon you. People are whispering. You're the talk of the town. You've been ostracized from the group, and all they do is stare.

Don't give up. All hope is not lost. Although you feel invisible, you are not invisible to God. Although you feel lonely, you have never been alone. God has been there through it all—sometimes walking beside you, while at other times carrying you. Like the impotent man, you have a choice. You can stay where people and circumstances have left you, or you can choose to *rise* above it all.

You are not just another number. You are not a label. You have a name, and your name is, Victory! I do not mean to suggest that your situation and circumstances will magically change in an instant, but how you see yourself can change that quickly. Stop viewing yourself as a loser, or hopeless, or doomed to fail. Choose to see what God sees. Everything He created was good and very good—and that includes you! You may be down today, but if you choose to keep pushing and persevering, it will absolutely change your perspective and give you a new outlook on life.

THE CHOICE IS YOURS!

Despite your past, you can choose a different future. You no longer have to remain in toxic relationships. You can choose to pray for strength and clarity to detach yourself from anything and anyone who threatens your health and sense of well-being. You can choose to say *no*. You do not have to accept what has been thrown at you. You are better than that, bigger than that, and stronger than that. Conversely, you can choose to say *yes*—yes to God's will for your life. Yes to blessings you can't begin to fathom. Yes to peace of mind.

Today can be the day that you choose to trust God. Consider everything you have been through. Think of all the tears you've cried and all the sleepless nights, the depression, the hopelessness, the powerlessness—what do you have to lose? Jesus is knocking at the doors of your heart. The enemy has you down for the count, but Jesus is kneeling right there beside you. It's as if He is saying that you do not have to stay down; you do not have to lose the final round. My friend, I pray that the words of Jesus are beginning to resonate inside of you: "Rise, take up thy bed, and walk" (John 5:8 KJV). We can trust God wholeheartedly because His Word declares, "I will never leave thee, nor forsake thee" (Hebrews 13:5 KJV). He also declares, "For with God nothing shall be impossible" (Luke 1:37 KJV). God wants for each of us to choose Him. My friend, do you hear His voice? Do you feel a tugging at your heart?

Today is the day you choose to get up. Today is the day you choose to walk away from whatever has you bound and walk toward the one who holds your future in the palm of His hand. Today's the day. The past is behind you. The pain is behind you. Failure is behind you. Today is the first day of the rest of your life. The choice is yours!

Sweet Surrender

There's something quite beautiful about surrender. There's no longer a need for resistance. The struggle is over. You can proudly wave the white flag and concede that you have gone as far as you can go. "Lord, I need you. I thought I could make it on my own. I thought I could make right everything that is wrong in my life. I thought I had the answers. But I am tired of feeling hopeless. I am tired of living in despair. I am sick and tired of being sick and tired—tired of the sadness, tired of the tears. I am tired of fighting this battle alone."

The act of surrender is sometimes viewed as defeat or as a sign of weakness. But surrendering to God is the most beautiful gift you will ever give yourself. It's acknowledging what God has always known: you need Him like you need air to breathe. Yet we find this so hard to admit and so hard to yield to.

For some reason, it's as if we would rather keep running into the same wall. It hasn't moved. It's still there. Yet we run full steam ahead toward it, time and time again. Walls of pain, walls of rejection, and walls of heartache. We dream of change; we dream of living different lives—lives without bars, lives without chains, lives where we can actually walk around without limping. And although it seems so very far away, the life we dream of is closer than we ever imagined. The life we dream of is on the other side of our saying, "Lord, I choose You."

How gracious is our God! He longs to hear these words fall from your lips. He has been waiting for you to come to this place of realization—this place of acceptance that He is everything you will ever need, that He is the only all-powerful and the only all-knowing. This place that is full of forgiveness and restoration. This place where grace abounds, and there is no judgment, no guilt, and no shame.

Everything that God does and everything that He allows is intentional. There is a reason behind everything you have been through. The trials were never meant to destroy you. They were heavy. They were painful. They were seemingly cruel at times. But they were never meant to destroy you. Have you ever considered that your trial was also for the benefit of someone else? There is a lesson in every trial and a purpose for every tear that falls from your eyes.

I remember playing kickball as a child and standing in a line with other classmates. It always felt good when classmates chose me to be on their team. Being chosen meant they felt I was good, had skill, and could add value to the team, as if they needed me on the team in order to win. In the same way, God wants to be our first choice. He wants us to know that He is good and righteous in all of His ways. He wants us to choose Him because He is the giver and sustainer of all life. Only He has the power and wisdom to add value and meaning to our lives. He wants us to realize that we need Him so we can win.

Surrendering to Him means we do not have to face life alone. People have walked in and out of our lives. They have abandoned their promises and vows and left us to fend for ourselves. Stress has consumed our lives. Our health has been affected; our emotions have become tattered and worn. We have stopped praying, we have stopped believing, and we have stopped fighting.

We have passively accepted the lies Satan has told us. It's as if he labeled us as pathetic, good for nothing, and hopeless, and we believed him. We were made to think we couldn't get up, so we stayed down. We believed we couldn't move, so we became paralyzed with fear. He convinced us that we would fail so we gave up on trying. He tricked us into believing that we had no choice, so we let him make the choice for us. We erroneously believed that our trials, hardships, and sicknesses were due to God's not loving us, so little by little, we fell out of love with God—our first love.

But, my friend, God's love has never changed. He has never stopped loving you. There has never been a time when He lost sight of you. Jesus knew exactly how long the impotent man had been sitting in that place. He may have been invisible to everyone else around him, but at no point was he ever invisible to Jesus. There is a time and a season for all things, and, thankfully for us, seasons change.

Life has not been easy. Not everything has gone as planned. There have been losses along the way. But you have a voice. You have a will. You have a choice. Surrendering your life and your situations to Christ is the beginning of peace. It is not at all a sign of weakness but a mark of strength.

Another favorite verse of mine is Romans 8:28 (KJV): "And we know that all things work together for good to them that love God, to them who are the called according to His purpose." I was anemic as a child, so my mom would give me the dreaded liquid iron, Geritol. It wasn't good *to* me, but it was good *for* me.

Whatever it is that you have gone through, suffered through, or plowed through was good for you. It didn't feel good; you never would have signed up for it, and maybe you wouldn't wish it on your worst enemy, but God has a way of making it work for your good.

Truth be told, we are not all that different from the impotent man. We can all identify with how he felt. We have all cried his same tears, and we have all felt the pangs of his frustration. But the good news is that *you* can also experience his victory. You no longer have to make excuses and play the blame game. You can seize this opportunity of a lifetime. God has spoken. The ball is in your court. *The Choice is Yours!* What's it going to be?

CPSIA information can be obtained
at www.ICGtesting.com
Printed in the USA
LVHW110259211220
674739LV00025B/160